LORD,
I Want To Tell You Something

LORD, I Want To Tell You Something

Chris Jones

Designed and Illustrated by
David Koechel

Augsburg Publishing House
Minneapolis, Minnesota

To Glyn and Owen
living with God in a boy's world

LORD, I WANT TO TELL YOU SOMETHING

For information address Augsburg Publishing
House, 426 South Fifth Street, Minneapolis,
Minnesota 55415.

MANUFACTURED IN THE UNITED STATES OF AMERICA

Contents

God, You're Great

No Matter What 11
Thank You for Skunks Even 12
The Dark Is Friendly 13
Jesus Lives 14
The Biggest Surprise of All 15
Secrets at the End of the Universe 17
Thank You for Being Everywhere 18
A Man-Made Brain 19
The Moon and Planet Earth 21
I Like Bugs 22

I'm Sorry, Lord

Messed-up Days 27
Far Away, but Still Close By 28
I Want to Be Like You 29
Win or Lose 30
Problem Thoughts 32
Friends Who Really Aren't 33
Feeling Different 35
How to Be Happy 36
I Blew It Again Today 37
A Special Time with You 38
Meanness Inside Me 40
It's Hard to Sit Still 41
Let's Clean Up the World 43
Acting Big 44

Thank You, Jesus

Sports Are Great 47
Laughing Makes Me Feel Good 48

Finger-Tapping, Foot-Stomping Music 49
Machines That Clatter and Whirr 51
Television Decisions 52
Forgotten Forever 53
Adventures in My Mind 55
Fun Times 57
When I'm Hungry 58
Everything That's Noisy 59
Camping Fun 61
Please Bless Mom 62
Dad Is Great 63
Frozen Lakes and Warm Mittens 65
Spring Is Here 66
I Wish It Could Be Forever 67
Tingling Noses 69
Kite-Flying Fun 70

Hear Me, Lord God

School Is Hard to Take 75
When We Go in the Car 76
Boys in the Bible 77
What Shall I Be? 78
Those Who Walk in Dark Alleys 79
What's It Like to Be Really Hungry? 81
When I'm Sick 82
One Special Friend 83
Do They Ever Have Any Fun? 84
Getting Along Together 85
Some Things Pull Me Away from You 86
Let Me Be Glad for Today 87
I Never Have Enough 89
People Are Kind 91
They Need Your Special Care 92
When Things Go Wrong 93
I'm Bigger than Cats and Dogs 95
Clean and New 96

Preface

Have you ever been told to stop talking? I was always in trouble at school for talking too much. Most people love to talk and we talk mostly to the people we love. We love Jesus and follow him, because he paid for our sins when he died on the cross. That's why we like to talk to him.

Prayer is just a religious word for talking to God, so don't let it put you off. You can talk to God. He likes you. He knows all about boys. Jesus was a boy once himself. Don't let the fact that he is God *worry* you; he *likes* you.

But the fact that he is God *should* have something to do with the way we talk to him. We don't talk to Mom and Dad the way we talk to our friends at school. We have a special love for them. We respect them and this shows in the way we talk to them.

So it is with God. We love and respect him and this shows in the way we talk to him. I don't mean we have to use 'thee' and 'thou,' 'art' and 'wert.' That's how people used to talk when the Bible was first translated into English many years ago. We don't talk that way today. Older people might pray that way, but perhaps you'd get mixed up if you did. So just talk to God the way you usually talk. That's fine with him. He hears you.

He hears you, but how does he answer you?

God has four ways of answering prayers. If he says *yes*, everything's fine. When he says *no*, that's hard to take. Sometimes his answer is *wait* and sometimes he says *stop praying and get going!*

The answer that's the hardest to understand is when God says *no*. We have to remember that God knows everything and he knows what's best. Sometimes we ask for things that just aren't good for us. We should remember too that God doesn't answer selfish prayers. If all we have to do is pray for everything we want, we would soon become lazy and greedy.

Sometimes when we think God is saying *no* to a prayer we should see if perhaps he is really saying *stop praying and get going!* God doesn't answer our prayers when we can answer them ourselves.

But prayer isn't only asking for something. We talk to Mom and Dad when we're happy, excited and even when we're miserable. We tell them we love them and we say we're sorry when things go wrong. We can talk to God about all those things too.

This book is just to get you started in talking to God. It is to show you that you don't have to pray like a grown-up. Just be yourself when you talk to God because God likes boys and especially he likes to answer your prayers.

God, You're Great!

1

No Matter What

Lord Jesus, thank you for loving me
even when I do things I shouldn't.
Thank you for loving me
because that means I can always trust you
to take care of me.
Thank you for loving me
because sometimes I feel like no one else does
and I feel lonely and unhappy.
Thank you for loving me
enough to die for me.

Thank You for Skunks Even

Thank you God, for puppies,
with soft ears and big sad eyes.
Thank you for *all* the furry things you make
like foxes, rabbits, squirrels, bear cubs—
skunks even.
I wish wild animals would be friendly
and skunks wouldn't smell,
so I could play with them too.
Thank you for all living things
the wild ones and the friendly ones too.

The Dark Is Friendly

Thank you for making the night, God.
It's fun to play out in the dark,
to run and hide or just kick a ball.
The dark is friendly,
and I like to look at the stars.
Thank you for night time, God,
for fun in the dark
and for time to sleep.

Jesus Lives!

Thank you Lord, for coming to earth,
for making people happy,
for making them well,
for teaching about God
and for dying on the cross.
But most of all, thank you
for coming alive again.
Now we can go to heaven
because you paid for our sins.
Thank you for that, Lord Jesus.

The Biggest Surprise of All

I'm so excited, Jesus!
Christmas is such a great time—
full of gifts and surprises.
But you were the biggest surprise of all
because no one thought you'd come
as a tiny baby
and be born in a poor place like a stable.
You were the best gift of all, too,
a gift from God to bring us life forever.
Thank you for being the biggest surprise
and the best gift.

Secrets at the End of the Universe

Great God, scientists are finding out
new things
about your universe everyday.
I can't figure out how long a light year is
yet my encyclopedia says
that some stars are billions
of light years away.
And you created all of them.
I wish I had a telescope so powerful
I could see to the end of the universe.
Then I could discover
some more of its secrets.
O God of the earth, galaxies,
and the universe
I praise you for your greatness.

Thank You for Being Everywhere

I don't understand how you can be
everywhere God,
but I'm glad you are
because that means you see everything
that happens to me—
even if I'm in the jungle,
under the ocean, on the moon
or just going to school,
and you can take care of me.
Thank you for being everywhere.

A Man·Made Brain

Computers are marvelous things, Lord.
I see them on TV
and they know all kinds of answers.
I'd love to push all the buttons
and see the flashing lights.
Computers can do just about anything,
they're almost human.
But that's the really marvelous thing, Lord,
to think that you made man
with such a brain
that he can almost make a brain himself.

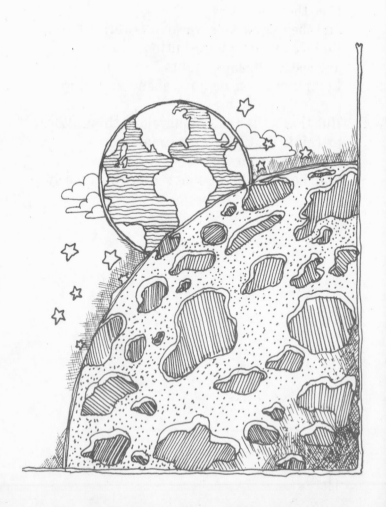

The Moon and Planet Earth

Great God, I'm glad you made the earth
the way you did.
The moon is empty with only rocks and dust,
but we have rivers, trees, and prairies,
deserts, canyons, flowers, and green grass.
The astronauts in their capsules say
the earth is full of color, the moon is not.
And so, O God,
for the beautiful planet Earth
you made for us,
I praise you.

I Like Bugs

Father, there are so many interesting kinds
of bugs.
You really did a good job
when you made them,
I mean like the way some caterpillars
change colors
to match the leaf they're on
so birds can't see them easily.
Or like the leaf hopper grub that stays cool
in a mess of spit
until it's ready to come out and hop.
Thank you for helping me to learn
all about bugs,
so I can see how great you are.
I'll try not to hurt them.

I'm Sorry, Lord

Messed Up Days

I'm sorry, Lord. It's been a bad day.
I've messed up so many things today.
Please wash away
all the wrong things I've said
and done and thought.
Thank you for your promise in the Bible
to forgive
because I know you will forgive me too.
So please hear me and help me
to make tomorrow a better day.

Far Away, but Still Close By

O God, today you seem so far away.
Even though I know you're listening
when I pray,
it doesn't feel like it.
Help me to remember
that you are always with me,
because I need you God.

I Want to Be Like You

Lord God, I want to be good like you
but often I'm not.
I wish I could love everyone, as you do,
but somehow I can't.
You are always kind,
and some days that's hard for me too.
But I know you are with me,
and if I listen
you will teach me to be good,
to love everyone,
and to be kind every day.

Win or Lose

I hate to lose a game, Father,
any kind of game.
I know I should play just for the fun of it,
but I feel awful when I lose.
Please help me not to get upset when I lose.
Make me a good sport
and help me to enjoy the game
whether I win or lose.

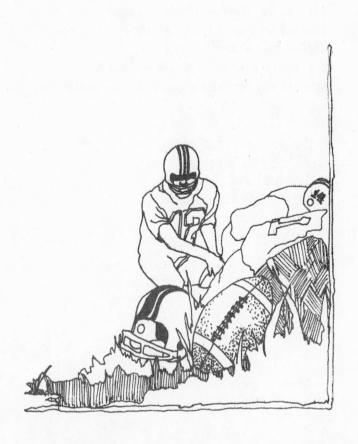

Problem Thoughts

Lord Jesus, I have this problem
with my thoughts.
Sometimes they just aren't good.
I make up jokes in my mind that I shouldn't
and sometimes I listen to others
telling bad jokes.
I wouldn't like it if Mom or Dad
or my teacher knew what I was thinking.
But Lord, *you* know,
and that makes me feel bad.
Help me to think about good things,
clean things, happy things,
so I don't have time
for the other kind of thoughts.

Friends Who Really Aren't

O God, I hate fighting with my friends,
but sometimes I get so mad
I could punch them in the nose—
like when they wreck my game,
or call me names,
or won't let me play with them.
Help me to remember that you love them
and help me love them too
even when they're mean to me.

Feeling Different

Lord, I hate to feel different,
like when I have to wear my boots
and the others aren't wearing theirs.
Sometimes I think they'll laugh at me.
I guess others feel like that, too.
I know you love everyone,
so help me be friendly and kind to everyone
even those who look different
because maybe their skin is a different color
or they speak with a different accent.
You love them even if their teeth stick out
or they have big ears,
or their clothes aren't very new.
Please forgive me
for making fun of other people.

How to Be Happy

Sometimes I feel crabby.
I don't know why, I just wake up that way.
Lord, how do I get to be happy?
Is it by being glad for what I have?
Or by obeying you?
Or maybe by making others happy?
Is it by remembering that you love me?
I guess it's all of these things.
Please help me to be happy, Lord,
and not crabby.

I Blew It Again Today

Well, Lord, I blew it again today, didn't I?
It's that bad temper of mine.
I feel unhappy now—and sorry too.
I get so mad if I don't get my own way
or if I have to do something
I don't want to do.
I think I should say I'm sorry.
Please help me, Lord,
when all that anger boils up inside me.

37

A Special Time with You

Lord, sometimes I don't want to
go to church.
There are so many fun things to do
here at home,
especially if I'm in the middle of something
important.
But I know that at church
I can spend a special time with you.
Even though you are with me all the time,
at church I can give you all my thoughts.
I can pray and worship you
without anything breaking in,
and that is special.
Forgive me for wanting that time
for myself.

Meanness Inside Me

Lord, I know sometimes I'm really mean.
I won't let some kids play with me
and my friends.
I play mean tricks on people.
I laugh at kids who aren't very smart
or who get the wrong answer in school.
I don't know why I do it, Lord.
It doesn't make me feel very good inside.
Please forgive me, Lord.
Take away the meanness inside me
and give me more of Jesus' love for others.

It's Hard to Sit Still

Lord, sometimes in church
I feel like giggling or playing around.
I don't mean to be rude to you, Lord.
It's just that some things seem funny,
and it's so hard to sit a long while.
I'm sorry, Lord.
I really want to worship you
and I *do* love you.

Let's Clean Up the World

Lord, sometimes I wonder
what the earth was like
when it was all new.
I wonder—and then I'm sad,
because I see your beautiful rivers
all brown and scummy,
and the lakes, slimy green
with old tires sticking out.
And I see junky cars piled in fields.
Sometimes I forget
and throw down empty pop cans
and candy wrappers, without thinking.
Lord, I'm sorry for the times
I spoil your world.
Show me what I can do
to make it beautiful again.

Acting Big

O Lord, sometimes I tell lies
because I've done something wrong,
or because I want to feel big.
I know I shouldn't, but it's hard not to—
especially if I think
I'm going to get into trouble.
Lord please remind me
the next time I want to tell a lie
and help me to tell the truth all the time.

Thank You, Jesus

3

Sports Are Great

Father, I love the feel of the hard-hit ball
slapping into my glove
before I fire it to third base.
I like to dribble a basketball
and toss it into the net
like it was nothing at all.
I like to clash sticks and zip across the ice
chasing the puck
until someone slaps it into the goal.
Lord, sports are great!
Thank you for all of them.

Laughing Makes Me Feel Good

O Lord, I like to laugh so hard
I fall on the floor.
Like when a clown gets a pie in the face
or a funny lady on TV loses her wig.
But I like it best of all
when Mom and Dad and I share a joke
and we all laugh.
That feels good inside.
Thank you, Lord, for good times like that.

Finger·Tapping,
Foot·Stomping Music

I like music, Lord—
finger-tapping, foot-stomping music—
guitars that twang, drums that thump,
and harmonicas that whine.
But most of all I like music when it's loud!
We've had music so long now,
you'd think we would have run out of tunes.
Thank you for all kinds of music,
even the kind Mom likes
and the brass bands Dad loves to hear.
It's good to have something for everybody.

Machines That Clatter
and Whirr

I like to watch all kinds of machines—
the power shovels that gouge great holes
and the earthmover that pushes hills away.
And then factory machines
with pistons, cogs, and wheels
that clatter and whirr,
doing the work of ten men or more.
Thank you, Lord, for machines
that make things quickly and easily
and for the men who invented them.

Television Decisions

Thank you God, for the happy hours I spend
watching TV.
I learn a lot of good things from it,
some bad things too, I guess—
like shooting, fighting, and killing.
Teach me which shows are good
and which are bad.
I like the exciting ones
and the funny ones too.
Help me choose the good shows,
the friendly, interesting, happy ones
that make me feel that way too.
And help me not to watch TV
when I should be doing something else.

Forgotten Forever

O God, thank you for forgiving
and forgetting my sins,
because some of the things I've done
I'll be real happy if no one ever remembers
them again.
Thank you for wiping them out, Jesus,
just like my teacher cleans the chalk board.
Now I can begin again with you helping me.

Adventures in My Mind

Thank you, Lord, for books.
I like my encyclopedias that tell me
where I can find an active volcano
and which animal runs the fastest.
Some books give diagrams and charts
and tell me how to make things.
But best of all I like the adventure books
that can take me in my mind
through jungles with snakes and bugs,
or investigating crimes,
or exploring unknown worlds under the sea.
Thank you Lord, that on a rainy day
I can curl up on my bed and read,
and go far away in my thoughts.

Fun Times

Thank you for fun, Father—
for running in the summer rain
with no shirt on,
for speeding on my bike,
for climbing trees,
and playing tag.
For secret hideouts and passwords,
and all the other fun things to do,
thank you, Father.

When I'm Hungry

Thank you for all the good things to eat—
like birthday cake,
hot dogs, corn chips, and bubble gum,
hamburgers, chicken drumsticks,
and french fries with salt and ketchup.
There are so many different kinds of food
I can't even think of all the ones I like best.
Thank you for everything
that tastes so good
and thank you for a good appetite.

Everything That's Noisy

Father, I love noise.
I love to stomp through the house
to yell at a ball game,
to turn up the TV,
and to hammer loud
when I'm making something.
I love to hear the big jetliners
roar overhead
or listen to the thump-thump
of the big drum in a parade.
Thank you for loud noises, Father,
and for the little ones too.
Thank you for good ears to hear a whisper
as well as the big drum.

Camping Fun

Thank you, Lord, for trails in the woods
and rocky cliffs to climb,
for tracking wild animals
and fishing in deep lakes,
for building campfires,
and lying quietly in my tent and listening
to the night noises.
For all camping fun I thank you, Lord.

Please Bless Mom

I'm sorry for the times I upset Mom,
for when I forget to do the things she asks
and when I talk back.
Help me to show her I love her
by keeping my room clean,
and taking out the garbage,
picking up my stuff,
and things like that.
Thank you Lord, for Mom.
Please bless her.

Dad Is Great!

Thank you, Lord, for my Dad.
He's great!
He fixes things like bikes and broken toys.
He plays games with me
and teaches me to play baseball.
He takes me different places,
and I feel good
just being with him.
Please bless him, Lord.

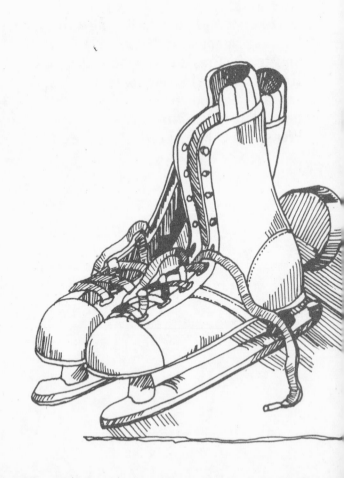

Frozen Lakes and Warm Mittens

Thank you, Lord, for snow
and hard frozen lakes to skate on,
for snowball fights, warm mittens,
scarves and boots.
Thank you for toboggans and skis
and steep hills to go down.
And thank you for fir trees
weighted down with heavy snow.
Thank you for winter, O Lord,
and thank you especially for dry clothes
and a warm home to come to when I'm cold.

Spring Is Here!

It smells so good outside today.
The snow's almost gone,
and the grass is squishy, wet, and muddy.
Now I can catch frogs and small silver fish
and splash in the puddles
when the rain has stopped.
Now I can play baseball again.
Thank you, God, for springtime,
when everything turns
from black and white
to green and yellow
and all my friends are out on their bikes
again.

I Wish It Could Be Summer Forever

I wish it could be summer forever.
It's so great not to have to wear a jacket
when I go out
and to go barefoot if I want to.
I can play out late after supper
because I don't have to get up for school.
That's what I like about summer, God—
just taking it easy,
under a tree,
or whacking a ball past third base.
Even if it's hot and sticky,
I can go swimming
or chew on an ice cube.
Thank you, Lord God,
for all the things I enjoy in the summer.

Tingling Noses

Thank you God, for the piles of fat
pumpkins at the store,
the leaves to kick around and roll in.
Thank you for the cold morning air
that makes my nose tingle as I go to school.
It's fun to watch my breath come out like
puffs of smoke,
to dress up in something scary
for Halloween,
or snuggle down in bed and listen to the rain
beating on my window.
Thank you for the fall.

Kite·Flying Fun

Thank you for windy, spring days
when I can fix my kite
and fly it in the strong gusts of wind.
The kite tugs so hard
until it's almost out of sight
and I run out of string.
That's when I feel I could just hang on
and drift away with it.
Thank you, God, for kite-flying fun.

Hear Me, Lord God

4

School Is Hard to Take

Lord, sometimes school is hard to take.
Often I don't feel like sitting that long.
I think some of the things I have to learn
are dumb.
I want to be outside playing football
or chasing other kids.
Some days I don't feel very thankful
for my teachers
even though they're good to me
and help me with my work.
You went to school, Jesus,
so you know how I feel.
Please help me do a good job
with my assignments
even when I don't feel like it.
And bless my teachers.
Help them to be patient.
And help me remember
all the things I'm supposed to.

When We Go in the Car

Lord, please keep us safe
when we go in the car.
Help Dad to drive carefully
so we don't have any accidents.
Sometimes we see smash-ups,
and then I'm scared it might happen to us.
So please keep us safe in the car.
Help me to be patient until we get there.

Boys in the Bible

Father, thank you for making sure
there were stories in the Bible about boys.
Joseph had a special coat
and was sold as a slave,
by his brothers.
Samuel heard you call him.
David killed Goliath,
and Daniel was kept in prison.
Help me to be forgiving like Joseph,
obedient like Samuel,
brave like David,
and faithful like Daniel.
O Father, make me a true follower of you.

What Shall I Be?

Lord Jesus, I can't decide what to be
when I'm grown-up.
Sometimes I think it must be neat
to be an astronaut, or a mechanic,
or a football player.
What do you think Lord?
I'm glad you know all about me
because you know what I can do best.
Guide me as I grow up
to do the work
you want me to do.

Those Who Walk In Dark Alleys

Go with the policemen each day, O Lord,
as they drive in their patrol cars
and break up fights,
as they walk in dark alleys
and hunt in old houses,
looking for criminals.
Please keep them safe.
Help them make good decisions
when they arrest someone.
Teach them to love you
and ask you to help them in their work,
because a policeman's job is especially hard.

What's It Like to Be Really Hungry?

I've seen some pictures of people
who are very poor.
They look skinny and sad.
I guess they were starving.
I've never been that hungry.
Please help the poor people, Jesus,
and show me how I can help them too.
Thank you that we have plenty to eat.

When I'm Sick

Jesus, when you were on earth
sick people came to see you
and you helped them.
I'm asking you to help me now,
because I'm sick too.
Show the doctor how to make me well again
and help me not to give Mom a hard time
if I need a shot or some medicine.

One Special Friend

Lord, please send me a friend,
one special, close friend
who can share my secrets.
David, in the Old Testament,
must have been so glad
to have a friend like Jonathan
when King Saul was chasing him.
Lord, could I have a friend like that?
We could go for bike rides together
or hunt frogs by the pond,
or just talk.
I'm glad I can talk to you, Lord,
and that you are my friend.
At least when I remember that,
I don't feel quite so lonely.

Do They Ever Have Any Fun?

It must be hard being the president, Lord.
I've seen him on TV
when he speaks to the nation.
There are lots of other men
who have important jobs too,
like governors and mayors,
senators and congressmen.
Do they ever have any fun, I wonder?
Lord, please help them
make wise and fair decisions.
May they always turn to you for help,
and may they have
some fun times too, Lord.

Getting Along Together

Dear Father, please teach everyone
how to get along
so that there will be no more
war and fighting.
Help everyone to love one another
because you love them.
And, Father, help me
to get along with others,
because when I don't, that is like war too.

Some Things Pull Me Away from You

Father, there are many wrong things
I sometimes want to do—
things that would pull me away from you.
I think it would make me
feel big to do them.
Then I could be one of the group.
It's hard to stand alone,
to be called chicken,
to say no.
Help me, O Father, to be strong.

Let Me Be Glad for Today

Father, I'm so bored.
I wish I had something exciting to do.
I've read all my books,
there's nothing exciting on TV,
I'm tired of playing games,
and I can't go outside because it's raining.
Help me to be glad for every hour—
even the boring ones.
O Lord, please show me how to make each
hour count.

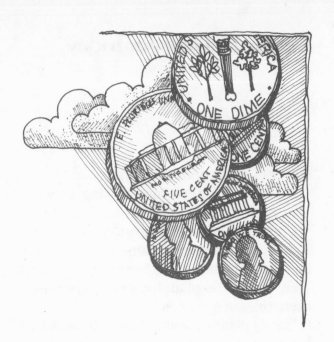

I Never Have Enough

I'm glad I have an allowance,
but somehow I never seem to have enough.
I spend it on things that don't last.
And really good things cost so much,
and it takes a long time to save up.
Even though money's good to have,
help me remember that it's not as important
as loving you.

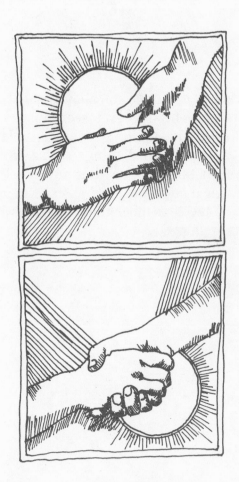

People Are Kind

O God, sometimes when I'm quiet
and I think about it,
I remember that some people
are really kind to me.
My teacher takes time
to explain things to me.
My friends share their candy with me.
The policeman takes care of me
if I get lost or hurt.
The neighbors are friendly.
Even strangers smile at me sometimes.
I think it must make you very happy
to see people love one another like that.
Help me show love
to other people too.

They Need Your Special Care

For people who lose their homes
in storms or floods,
for those men hurt in the war
who have to live with their wounds,
for those with illnesses
the doctors can't help,
for those whose minds are sick
and can't live normally,
and for sick children
who may never get better,
dear Jesus, I pray.
Take special care of them,
just as you did when you were on earth.

When Things Go Wrong

Sometimes I make up my mind
about doing something
and then maybe it rains,
or I have to go somewhere with Mom.
Sometimes Dad promises
to take me somewhere
and I get sick—or Dad has to work,
and then we can't do what we planned.
Lord, then I feel sad and angry
at the same time,
but please remind me to be thankful
for all the times
my plans go right.

I'm Bigger Than Cats and Dogs

Let me be kind to animals, Lord.
They can't talk back,
and I'm much bigger and stronger
than some of them
like cats and dogs,
rabbits, frogs, hamsters, squirrels and birds.
You made them all
and they make the world interesting.
Teach me not to tease them or hurt them
with rocks or BB guns.
Remind me to take care of my pets
because they need me.

Clean and New

O God, thank you for clean new things,
like a new notebook
with smooth, white pages,
clean sheets on my bed that smell so good,
a new pair of pants that look great,
or even a fresh patch of snow
that hasn't been stepped on.
It's fun to be the first one
to make footprints in it.
God, sometimes I spoil new things,
like that new notebook
and this new day.
Thank you for forgiving me for yesterday,
and thank you for each new day in my life.